CHRISTMAS PROGRAMS for the CHURCH Number 12

Compiled by
Jacqueline Westers

STANDARD PUBLISHING
Cincinnati, Ohio

8612

ISBN: 0-87239-252-X

Contents

This Same Jesus

Kathleen E. Snyder

Cast: Anchorman
Reporter
First Shepherd
Angel
Mary
Joseph
Angel Host (or Angel Choir)
Second Shepherd
Wise-men (optional)
Young Child (optional)
Third Shepherd
Fourth Shepherd
Extra People (number optional)

(NOTE: If desired, some participants may assume more than one role.)

Setting: On one side of the stage and at the rear should be a cross, prominent but as if in the distance. On the other side (rear) should be a tomb, with a "stone" in the doorway. If possible, there should be a curtain or screen that can be drawn or removed and then replaced. Anchorman may be off to one side, on or off the stage. Anchorman and Reporter should have microphones.

(*As scene opens, First Shepherd is seated contemplating the cross and tomb.*)

ANCHORMAN (*into mike*): This is your anchorman (*name*), coming to you from station (*name of church*) on this (*date*) day of December, (*year*). We have a special report of a new

time machine, which has just been perfected by Dr. Dudley
Tools. This machine will allow people to go back in time.
One of our own reporters has volunteered to be the first-
time traveler into time past. We understand he is being
sent to Bethlehem for a firsthand report on the birth of
Christ. We might actually get an interview with one of the
Wise-men, or perhaps with even Mary herself! *(Cups hand
over one ear.)* Come in, *(name of Reporter),* come in. Can
you hear me?

REPORTER *(entering):* This is *(name).* Yes, I can hear you,
but I think someone made a big mistake. *(Looking around)*
This sure isn't a manger in Bethlehem! It looks more like
something I read about happening some thirty-three years
later.

ANCHORMAN *(a little flustered):* My goodness! Stay with us,
friends; we'll try to get this problem ironed out. In the
meantime, *(Reporter),* since we're on the air, see if you can
find someone who might remember something about the
birth of Jesus.

REPORTER: Right-o! *(Going over to First Shepherd)* Pardon
me, but was someone crucified there recently *(indicating
cross)?*

FIRST SHEPHERD *(without looking up):* Yes, many people
have been crucified on such crosses by the Romans. Here is
the tomb where they say Jesus of Nazareth was buried
after He was crucified.

REPORTER: Yes, I seem to remember something about that.
But say, can you tell me anything about the birth of Jesus?
I understand that's quite a story.

FIRST SHEPHERD: Oh, yes, that *is* quite a story! I remember
it so well, but you must realize that it actually started
many, many years before His actual birth. The prophets of
old had spoken of the coming of the Messiah, how He
would be born of a virgin, of His ministry on earth, and
even of His suffering for our sins.

REPORTER: Yes, yes, but what about the actual birth? Can
you tell me anything about it?

FIRST SHEPHERD: Well, it all started one day in Nazareth,
when the angel Gabriel appeared to a young woman
named Mary. At that time she was engaged to Joseph, who
was a good man.

(During this speech, pull curtain over cross and tomb. Mary enters. Then Angel enters and Mary appears frightened. While curtain is pulled, set up a manger scene behind it, perhaps at the side where the cross is placed.)

ANGEL: Do not be afraid, Mary, for you have found favor with God. He has chosen you to be the mother of His Son, and you shall call His name Jesus.

MARY: But how can this be?

ANGEL: The Holy Spirit will come upon you, and therefore the child will be called holy, the Son of God.

(Angel and Mary leave.)

REPORTER: Wow! That must have been a surprise for Mary. Was she very upset?

FIRST SHEPHERD: Oh, no, she was happy for the Lord's will to be done. But with Joseph, her betrothed, it was quite different at first, for he didn't understand. He was a just and good man, and he planned to just quietly divorce Mary. But as he thought about this, the angel appeared to him in a dream.

(During this speech, Joseph enters and lies down; then Angel enters.)

ANGEL: Joseph, do not be afraid to take Mary as your wife. The child she is to bear is of the Holy Spirit. You shall call the child's name Jesus, for He will save His people from their sins.

(Angel and Joseph leave.)

FIRST SHEPHERD: When Joseph wakened, he obeyed and took Mary for his wife.

REPORTER: Hmm. But you said this all happened in Nazareth. I thought Jesus was born in Bethlehem.

FIRST SHEPHERD: That is true, and it happened this way: When the time was near for Mary to have the baby, Caesar Augustus issued the decree that all the people should be counted for a taxation. This required everyone to be recorded in the place of his nativity. Since Joseph was of the family of David, he and Mary had to travel from Nazareth to Bethlehem. While they were there the time came for Mary to have the baby.

(Pull curtain to reveal the manger scene with Joseph, Mary, and the child, or doll.)

Because of the census there was no room for them in the inn, so they found shelter in a stable. Mary wrapped her newborn Son in swaddling clothes and laid Him in a manger.

REPORTER: Imagine! Our Lord was laid in a feeding trough for animals! What happened next?

(Draw curtain over manger scene. As Shepherds enter at one side of stage, Reporter and First Shepherd move to opposite side.)

FIRST SHEPHERD: This is where I first learned what was happening, although I was acquainted with the Scriptures and knew the prophecies. I was a shepherd, and my friends and I were watching our sheep in a field of Judea, when suddenly a light shone upon us and an angel appeared. It was really frightening!

(During this speech the Angel enters and the Shepherds show fright. Spotlights may be used, if desired.)

ANGEL: "Fear not: for, behold, I bring you good tidings of great joy, which shall be to all people. For unto you is born this day in the city of David a Saviour, which is Christ the Lord. And this shall be a sign unto you; Ye shall find the babe wrapped in swaddling clothes, lying in a manger." (Luke 2:10-12)

(Other Angels enter and stand with Angel. If this is an Angel Choir, they may sing a stanza and chorus of "Angels We Have Heard on High"; if they are to speak, they will quote Luke 2:14.)

FIRST SHEPHERD: Suddenly it seemed that the whole earth and heavens were filled with angels, and all of them praising God.

(Angels leave after song or speech.)

SECOND SHEPHERD: This is a marvelous revelation from God!

THIRD SHEPHERD: We must obey the angel. Let us go to Bethlehem and see this thing that has happened.

(Shepherds leave and situate themselves around the manger scene, behind curtain.)

FIRST SHEPHERD: We hurried to Bethlehem and searched till we found Mary and Joseph, and the babe lying in the manger. When we saw Him, we told everyone what the angel had said about the child. Everyone was amazed with our story.

(Pull curtain to reveal the manger scene with the shepherds worshiping.)

REPORTER *(in awe):* Wow! I should think so! You are one of the actual shepherds who saw the Christ child! You must be very proud of that.

FIRST SHEPHERD: I just feel very humble that God chose me to be among the first to receive the announcement of His Son's birth and to see Him.

(Draw curtain over manger scene.)

REPORTER: Well, and now I guess this is where the Wise-men came into the picture, isn't it? I understand that the star led them to the manger about the same time you got there.

FIRST SHEPHERD *(surprised):* The Wise-men? Oh, my no! It was some time later that they came. The star led them to a house where Joseph, Mary, and the child were staying.

(If the scene of the Wise-men is used, Mary, Joseph, and Young Child enter and stand together. Then Wise-men enter at appropriate time, kneel, and offer gifts. Then they all leave, and curtain is pulled to show original scene.)

When they entered the house and saw Jesus, they fell down and worshiped Him. Then they offered Him gifts of gold, frankincense, and myrrh.

REPORTER: What a story! I didn't realize that the Wise-men weren't led to the manger. But, may I ask, if Jesus was crucified and buried, why are you still here?

FIRST SHEPHERD: When John the Baptizer came to the wilderness, preaching and baptizing, I knew of him. He spoke of the Christ who was to come after him, and I was sure that this was He whom we saw as an infant many years before. Then, some weeks ago, there was a Man who came and stayed for a time in the same wilderness where John preached. It was there I saw Jesus again. Someone said, and we all agreed, that John did no miracle, but all he had said was true of this Man, and we believed in Him. You see, Jesus' birth was proclaimed by angels. He was declared the Savior, Christ the Lord. God sent Him, and I'm sure that His was a special work for God. According to the Scriptures He was to suffer and die, and yet I cannot believe that it was all to end—here—like this *(indicating tomb)*.

(Toward the end of this speech people start gathering at the tomb.)

SECOND SHEPHERD: He is risen! He is risen! Jesus who was crucified has risen from the grave!

THIRD SHEPHERD: We have come from the city where we heard one named Peter proclaim that Jesus died for our sins, but He arose from the dead and is ascended to Heaven. Glory be to God in the Highest!

FOURTH SHEPHERD: He who was sent from God is now returned to God. Praise the Lord!

FIRST SHEPHERD: It is the fulfillment of the Scriptures. It is the same Jesus we saw on that night so long ago. Once more, we must tell everyone!

(All leave except Reporter.)

REPORTER *(facing audience)*: Ladies and gentlemen, the modern world has just witnessed the most tremendous moment in history. The story is just out that Jesus Christ has risen from the dead! I don't know what more there is to say, except that I know now that I want to find out more about this Man. Back to you, *(Anchorman)*. *(Leaves.)*

ANCHORMAN: Well, there you have it, ladies and gentlemen. Actually, it seems we received more than we requested. This Christmas story seems to have started a whole chain of events, all connected with this Christ child. Well, I see our time has run out. Station *(name of church)* wishes to thank you all for tuning in on our special. And now, from all of us here, a very Merry Christmas!

A Present-day Play

To the World With Love

The Seeker's Class
of the Christian Endeavor United Methodist Church

Cast: Grandmother Jones
       Grandfather Jones
       Mother (Helen)
       Father (Jim)
       Bob
       Beth
       Fred (Bob's friend)
       Boss
       Doctor
       Voice in the Box

Setting: A living room or family room. The stage should be divided (roughly) in two. A box, large enough for a person to be inside, is used as a divider, placed at front and center. It is to be wrapped like a Christmas gift, and tagged in large letters, "To the World With Love." On one side of the stage at the rear is a trimmed Christmas tree, and enough furnishings to seat six persons. Under the tree should be these wrapped gifts: a watch, a mixer, a briefcase, and an afghan. The other half of the stage at the rear is to be used for flashbacks in the action. In this area should be a desk with a small pad and pencil on top or in a drawer. Lights are used on one side or the other as directed. There should be a spotlight on the box throughout, and on the individuals as they come forward.

(*As scene opens, the family is in place with some gifts already opened. Everyone is "frozen" in position, as in a picture until the lights go on. After a moment, Mother hands Father the wrapped briefcase.*)

FATHER (*when gift is opened*): Oh, this is just fine, honey. I need a new briefcase for the office. Just great. *(He goes to front of stage and the rest of family "freeze" as lights go off. Talking to himself and to audience)* Just fine? Not really. I get more and more things, and better positions, yet something is wrong. Lately my life has become so monotonous—get up, go to work, come home, eat, and go to bed, day after day. The few pleasures I enjoy—golf, TV, fishing—are losing their appeal. They don't seem to satisfy, somehow. My kids are growing up and I'm starting to think of retirement and growing old. Even my job—I used to relish that, but now even that has lost its importance. *(Moving to other side of stage, as lights go on there and Boss enters)* Why, just the other day,

BOSS: Jim, we have a report here that must be done by 5:30 tonight. If this is turned in on time and approved, we have the best chance of receiving a government grant, and, of course, that could mean a nice fat bonus for you. *(Hands a paper to Father and leaves.)*

FATHER *(turning to audience)*: A nice fat bonus! What good will that do me later? I have plenty of money now, and still my life is empty. What do I care if the company receives that grant or not? There just has to be more to Christmas than what this briefcase means.

(As the Box begins to speak, Father acts surprised, then nods his head in agreement.)

BOX: Jesus Christ once said that He came to bring you life more abundant. He can offer you a purpose for being alive. He took away that hopeless, humdrum existence and replaces it with a life of excitement, adventure, and joy. Through Christ you can experience a day-by-day fellowship with an all-loving and all-knowing God. You have the privilege of putting your faith in Him, trusting Him daily, through good and bad times. Only with Him will you find the abundant and meaningful life.

(Lights off that side as Father returns to family side. As the lights come on that side, Family moves again and Father gives Mother her gift.)

MOTHER *(when gift is opened)*: Thank you so much. This is just what I need. It's beautiful. *(Family freezes as Mother comes forward and lights go off.)* Yes, thanks a lot. It is just what I need, something to do more work with. It seems that all I do is cook and bake, clean and shop. I do it all. Fight the hustle and bustle of Christmas shopping, sending, wrapping, and all the cooking. Well, sometimes I wonder if it's appreciated. No one seems to care or even notice. It makes you wonder if it's all worth it. *(Goes to other side of stage as lights go on there. Goes to desk and takes pad and pencil, as if making a grocery list.)*

BOB *(entering):* Hi, Mom. Did you get my football uniform ready?

MOTHER: Yes, it's ready, up in your room.

BOB: Great! I'd better hurry and get ready. Oh, Mom, can you take me to the school right after supper? I need to be there at 6:30 for practice.

MOTHER: I guess so. That means an early supper, but at least I'm glad you told me in time.

(Bob leaves and Beth enters.)

BETH: Love to help you with the cleaning, Mom, but I gotta go to Sandy's. I promised to help her with her homework. See you later. *(Starts to leave, then stops.)* Oh, yeah, I promised our 4H group that you'd bake cookies for our Christmas party tomorrow. And did you get the gift for my gift exchange? And don't forget it has to be wrapped. Thanks, Mom. See ya! *(Leaves.)*

MOTHER: Well, it seems there is never an end to it, and everyone is always too busy to help.

BOX: Jesus Christ came and gave you the greatest gift of all. His Word tells you to cast all your cares upon Him, for He cares for you. No one ever cared for you as Jesus does. He says that if you take His yoke and learn of Him, you will find rest for your soul. As you believe in Him and trust Him, you will find you can do all things through Christ who gives you strength. Leave your burdens with Him. Through Him you will receive the peace and joy you search for. These things are not of this world, but through Jesus Christ, who came to this world as the Savior and Prince of Peace. Yes, you can build your life and your home on this solid rock, or you can leave it in the sand of indifference or disbelief. The choice is yours.

(Lights off on that side as Mother, Bob, and Beth return to family scene. When they are situated there, the lights come on, and they move again. Bob is given his gift.)

Bob *(when gift is opened):* Wow, a watch! This is just what I wanted! Thank you; it's really great. *(Comes forward and family freezes.)* It's great all right. Just what I needed to remind me that the time for graduation is near, and then what? I haven't found out who I am yet, never mind the purpose for my life. I have no idea in what direction I'm going after school, and it really upsets me. Just the other day at school—

(Lights go off and Bob goes to other side of stage where lights come on. Fred enters.)

FRED: Hey, Bob, did you hear about Ralph Smith? You remember him; he graduated last year.

BOB: Yes, I remember him. He was a great football player—played on the varsity team. What about him?

FRED: Well, he went off to college, and then he got hooked on drugs. Last week they found him in his room, suffering from an overdose, and he died in the hospital.

BOB *(shaking head):* And everybody predicted that Ralph probably would go on to such great things, and really be somebody.

FRED: Yes, but I heard that he has been really down—not doing well in college, not making the college team, plus the money problems. He had a lot of pressures, and too much for him, I guess. *(Leaves.)*

BOX: God's Word says, "Trust in the Lord with all thine heart; and lean not unto thine own understanding. In all thy ways acknowledge him, and he shall direct thy paths." Jesus said, "I am the way, the truth, and the life." He is the answer to all your problems. He knows your needs and He has the plan and direction for your life. He loves you, Bob Jones! God sent Him into the world to save the world, and this means He sent Jesus for you, because He loves you. When you accept this, you will find the joy of Christmas and the right direction for your life. If you live for Jesus, lean on Him and trust Him, He will do all this for you, and more. The choice is yours; He is knocking. Won't you let Him into your heart?

(Lights off and Bob returns to family, where lights come on. Grandfather receives his gift.)

GRANDFATHER *(after gift is opened):* Thanks, children; I'll sure use this. *(To audience as others freeze)* Yeah, I'll use this. Seems I won't have a choice. Just get to be a certain age or have one setback, and you find yourself on the shelf. *(Goes to other side of stage, where lights come on.)* Just like the doctor said the other day when I went for my checkup.

DOCTOR *(entering, carrying a folder):* Well, Frank, the results of the tests show that you did suffer a mild stroke. You won't require hospitalization, but you will need to take this medication. *(Hands Grandfather a bottle or a paper.)* You are going to have to take it easy from now on, Frank. I would advise you to let your family help you more, instead of trying to do everything yourself. *(He leaves.)*

BOX: Is the doctor's advice a burden to you, Frank? Turn to Jesus, who said, "Let not your heart be troubled," and "Come unto me, all ye that labor and are heavy laden, and I will give you rest." The rest that Jesus has for you will give you peace of mind. It will take away your anxiety about growing old, and give you the assurance of eternal life. But you must have faith in Him and accept Him as your Savior.

(Grandfather returns to family as lights go off where he was and come on over family scene.)

BETH: Grandma, Christmas always seems so special to you. Your feeling toward it is so different from ours. Just what makes it different for you?

BOB: Yeah, but not only Christmas. Grandma always seems so happy. How come?

GRANDMOTHER: Christmas presents always remind me of God's Gift to the world—His only Son, Jesus. But He was a special gift to me years ago. When I became a Christian as a young girl, He gave me direction as I followed His leading. He gave me the love and patience I needed as a young wife and mother, and He gave me a real purpose for my life. Now that I'm getting old, the most precious thing of all is knowing that I'm closer to eternal life with Him, and there is no fear of death.

BETH: That is great. I'd like to have that happiness too.

BOB: You mean that Jesus really can let me know who I am, and where I am going?

FATHER: Can Jesus give me more to life than just the rat race I'm in?

MOTHER: And there really is more to look forward to than more cleaning, cooking, and dirty dishes?

GRANDFATHER: Ethel, I've been the one who has been worrying about how little time we may have left together. I'm beginning now to see the reason behind your peace. Before I was envious of it and sometimes it made me mad. And of course I wouldn't listen when you tried to talk about it. But I'm ready now.

BETH: Yes, Grandma, I think we all are. What do we have to do?

GRANDMOTHER: Well, Beth, you must first realize that salvation is a free gift, because it was bought by the Lord Jesus. The Bible says, "By grace are ye saved through faith; and that not of yourselves: it is the gift of God." When a person realizes, "This gift is for me; Jesus died for me because He loved me," he repents of his sins and seeks forgiveness. Jesus already is knocking at the door of your heart. He says, "Behold, I stand at the door and knock; if any man hear my voice, and open the door, I will come in to him, and will sup with him, and he with me." This is receiving Jesus as your own personal Savior. We must ask Him in; He will not enter otherwise. When we do this, we are ready to confess Him as ours and we will seek to please Him and obey Him.

FATHER: Well, maybe we should begin by going to church together next Sunday.

GRANDMOTHER: You don't have to wait until Sunday to begin, Jim. We can begin by praying right now.

(All bow their heads as lights go off.)

A Departmental Program
Featuring a Speaking Choir

Rejoice, for the Light Has Come

Irma Dietz

PRELUDE
HYMN *(by congregation):* "O Come, All Ye Faithful"
WELCOME and PRAYER *(by minister or leader)*
SCRIPTURE READING *(by speaking choir)*
  All: The voice of him that crieth in the wilderness,
  Male Solo: Prepare ye the way of the Lord, make straight in
    the desert a highway for our God.
  All Girls: Every valley shall be exalted,
  All Boys: And every mountain and hill shall be made low:
  All Girls: And the crooked shall be made straight,
  All Boys: And the rough places plain:
  Female Solo: And the glory of the Lord shall be revealed,
  All: And all flesh shall see it together.   *(Isaiah 40:3-5)*
THE LIGHT OF THE WORLD *(by Reader and Choir)*
  Scripture Reader: There was a man sent from God, whose
    name was John. The same came for a witness, to bear
    witness of the Light, that all men through him might be-
    lieve (John 1:6, 7).
  Choir: "The Light of the World Is Jesus"
SCRIPTURE READING *(by Speaking Choir)*
  All: The people that walked in darkness have seen a great
    light: they that dwell in the land of the shadow of death,
    upon them hath the light shined.
  Male Solo: For unto us a child is born, unto us a son is given:
    and the government shall be upon his shoulder:
  Female Solo: And his name shall be called Wonderful,
  Another Male Voice: Counselor,

Another Female Voice: The mighty God,
Male Voice: The everlasting Father,
Female Voice: The Prince of Peace.   *(Isaiah 9:6)*

(Indicate a lapse of time by a musical interlude, blinking of lights, or a sign.)

RECITATION: "Hope"

The world in deepest darkness lay,
  No ray of light was shining;
And few there were who seemed to care
  About a silver lining.
Behind the cloudy skies appeared
  A glimmer, Faint but cheering;
The time the prophets had foretold
  Was very surely nearing.

Then one day the Messiah came!
  The promised King of glory,
God's Son, the Savior of mankind,
  Foretold in song and story.
The faithful hearts rejoiced to see
  The star of His appearing;
For at His birth hope, too, was born,
  The light of God's love bringing.

Hope! How wonderful to know
  The curtain of Heaven lifted;
Thus, after many silent years
  The clouds had suddenly shifted.
The Light, oh, Hope of ages past,
  To us, too, has been given,
To lead the yearning souls of earth
  To His glad light of Heaven.

FINGER PLAY *(by little children):* "It's Christmas Day"

My eyes see things that tell me
  (Thumbs and forefingers framing eyes)
This is Christmas Day.
My ears hear things that tell me
  (Hands behind ears)
This is Christmas Day.
The Bible says, long years ago
  (Hands together, then open)

The mother, Mary, smiled for joy,
    (Hands wreathing smiles)
For God had sent a baby boy
    (Make cradle of arms and rock)
That first Christmas Day.
    (Follow with children's favorite carol.)

SONG *(by Choir):* "O Little Town of Bethlehem"

SCRIPTURE READING *(by Speaking Choir)*

All: And there were in the same country shepherds abiding in the field, keeping watch over their flock by night.

Female Solo: And, lo, the angel of the Lord came upon them, and the glory of the Lord shone round about them;

All: And they were sore afraid.

Female Solo: And the angel said unto them,

Male Solo: Fear not: for, behold, I bring you good tidings of great joy, which shall be to all people. For unto you is born this day in the city of David a Saviour, which is Christ the Lord. And this shall be a sign unto you; Ye shall find the babe wrapped in swaddling clothes, lying in a manger.

Female Solo: And suddenly there was with the angel a multitude of the heavenly host praising God, and saying,

All: Glory to God in the highest, and on earth peace, good will toward men.   *(Luke 2:8-14)*

EXERCISE *(by four boys):* "A Shepherd Boy I'd Like to Be"

SHEPHERD SCENE *(pantomime or slide)*

First Boy: The shepherds on the Bethlehem hills
    Watched their flocks at night,
When suddenly appeared to them
    A bright and holy light.
A shepherd boy I'd like to be,
That wondrous light I'd like to see.

Second Boy: God sent His angel to announce
    That He had sent His Son
Down to the earth, and bringing peace,
    Goodwill to everyone.
A shepherd boy I'd like to be;
Maybe the angel would speak to me!

Third Boy: And suddenly with the angel
    There appeared the heavenly throng.
Their voices swelled in praise to God
    With their hallelujah song.

A shepherd boy I'd like to be,
    If angels would sing their song for me!
Fourth Boy: The shepherds journeyed to Bethlehem
    To find the little child;
    In the manger, as the angel had said,
    Lay the Christ child, meek and mild.
    A shepherd boy I'd like to be;
    The little baby I'd like to see.

SONG *(by Choir):* "While Shepherds Watched Their Flocks"

SCRIPTURE READING *(by Speaking Choir)*

Female Voices: And it came to pass, as the angels were gone away from them into heaven, the shepherds said one to another,

Male Voices: Let us now go even unto Bethlehem, and see this thing which is come to pass, which the Lord hath made known unto us.   *(Luke 2:15, 16)*

NATIVITY SCENE *(pantomime or slide)*

SONG *(by congregation):* "Silent Night"

SOLO *(vocal or instrumental):* "O Holy Night"

RECITATION: "We'll Worship Him"
    We all are glad for Christmastime,
        That happy time of year,
    With gifts and treats and gatherings,
        And friends we love so dear.
    But we will still remember
        That this is Jesus' day,
    And we will seek to honor Him
        In all we do and say.
    And so we ask you earnestly
        That you, too, will remember
    To worship Jesus on His day,
        The twenty-fifth of December.

SONG *(by Choir):* "O Come, All Ye Faithful"

SCRIPTURE READING *(by Speaking Choir)*

All Male Voices, except three: Now when Jesus was born in Bethlehem of Judea in the days of Herod the king, behold, there came wise men from the east to Jerusalem, saying,

Three Male Voices: Where is he that is born King of the Jews? for we have seen his star in the east, and are come to worship him.

Female Voices: And when they were come into the house,

they saw the young child with Mary his mother, and fell
down, and worshipped him:
 All Male Voices: And when they had opened their treasures,
they presented unto him gifts; gold, and frankincense, and
myrrh. *(Matthew 2:1, 2, 11)*
SOLO *(violin or other instrument):* "Star of the East"
SCENE OF WISE-MEN *(pantomime or slide)*

(In this scene, if pantomimed, have the Wise-men come down an aisle from the rear of the auditorium and stop at the stage. The program may end here with the congregation singing "Joy to the World," followed by a benediction.)

RECITATION *(by Beginners):* "Gifts for Jesus"
 First Child (showing bell): The gift I have for Jesus is this
pretty silver bell; it will ring the happy tidings, and the
Christmas story tell.
 Second Child (showing candle): The gift I have for Jesus is
the light this candle gives; I'll shine my light around the
world to tell it Christ still lives.
 Third Child (showing star): The gift I have for Jesus is this
star that shines so bright, that all the world will know His
love this happy Christmas night.
 Fourth Child (showing heart): The gift I have for Jesus is my
heart, loving and true; Friends, why don't you give the
Savior your heart too?

(Follow with a favorite carol of the children.)

CLOSING THOUGHTS *(by minister or leader):* The Christmas
songs and Scriptures, the recitations and scenes of the
nativity, have recalled to mind the story of the babe in the
manger of Bethlehem. If the story of the coming of the Son
of God touches your heart, think of Him no longer as a
babe in the manger. Remember that He was willing, not
only to enter this world, but to die for our sins on Calvary's
cross. One day He is coming in power and glory to claim
His own, and we will be with Him forever.
SCRIPTURE READING *(by Speaking Choir)*
 Male Solo: Surely I come quickly:
 All: Amen. Even so, come, Lord Jesus.
CLOSING SONG *(by congregation):* "One Day"
BENEDICTION

The Christmas Story—Today!

Ramona Warren

Cast: Youth 1 (Mary)
Youth 2 (Joseph)
Youth 3 (Gabriel)
Youth 4 (Innkeeper)
Youth 5 (Innkeeper's Wife)
Youth 6 (Elisabeth)
Director
Luke
First Shepherd
Second Shepherd
Third Shepherd
First Wise-man
Second Wise-man
Third Wise-man
Herod
Chief Priest
Young Child
Youth Choir or Chorus

NOTE: Characters 1 through 6 have dual roles, identified by numbers in the opening scene and by names afterward. Other roles may be doubled also, if desired.

Staging: If possible, use four spotlights: one at center stage, one at front stage; the third at the left or right side exit (for scenes at door); and the fourth at extreme right or left below the stage. The choir or chorus may occupy the choir loft, a balcony, or sit at the back of the auditorium. If a choir is not used, a group of "angels" is needed for the shepherd scene. A tape recorder or phonograph may be used for the last song, with the cast singing "Joy to the World" as they leave.

Props: The only props needed are a chair, a pulpit or music stand, and the spotlights. No scenery or costumes are required.

Setting: The pulpit or stand and the chair are placed slightly to one side of stage.

(As the play opens, characters 1 through 6 enter. All others except the Choir occupy the front row of the auditorium.)

YOUTH 3: I hope we'll be doing a different kind of program for Christmas this year!

YOUTH 2: So do I!

YOUTH 5: Well, you know there is only one Christmas story.

YOUTH 3: I know, but I'm tired of the same old pageant, with angels in sheets and shepherds in bathrobes.

YOUTH 4: Remember last year's?

YOUTH 6: I'd rather forget it. It was a bummer.

YOUTH 1: All the shepherds but one got sick.

YOUTH 3: The Christmas tree fell over, right in the most serious part of the program.

YOUTH 4: And I forgot my lines!

YOUTH 5: I still say there's only one Christmas story. Why fight the system?

(Director enters, carrying stack of scripts, and goes to pulpit or stand.)

DIRECTOR *(looking around):* Everyone here? Good; let's get started. *(Hands out scripts to others on stage.)*

YOUTH 1: What do we have to do this year?

DIRECTOR: This is a little different program from what we usually do. I think you're going to like it.

YOUTH 3: You mean we're not going to do the Christmas story?

DIRECTOR: It's the Christmas story, but the Christmas story today.

(Participants from the front row come to front of stage to receive their scripts from Director, who keeps speaking.)

We will have no scenery, very few props, and no costumes.

YOUTH 4: Hurray!

YOUTH 2: Sounds great!

DIRECTOR: The play is written in today's language, and what we want is improvisation and strong acting. You must make the audience believe you are the character you portray without the help of a costume, sets, or props. If you forget your lines, improvise!

YOUTH 6: What about lights?

DIRECTOR: We'll have spots. They will be very important to the presentation. *(Returns to pulpit or stand to explain the setting.)* Some people think that Luke obtained his information for the story of Jesus' birth directly from Mary; therefore our play begins with a flashback, with Luke interviewing Mary. I have marked the roles with your names and stage directions, so we can begin.

(Everyone leaves except Mary and Luke. Characters in the front row move to stage entrance to wait for cues. They leave their scripts backstage. Luke places a chair at center stage for Mary. Stage lights are off, except for a spotlight on Mary. Choir, Chorus, or instrument may provide a musical interlude for change of scene. "Silent Night" would be appropriate.)

LUKE *(approaching Mary):* Mary, please tell me all you remember about Jesus' birth.

MARY: Remember? I remember everything, every detail.

LUKE: I'd like you to tell me about it, if you will.

(Luke moves out of spotlight. Mary comes to front of stage.)

MARY: I was just a young girl when Joseph and I became engaged. One day as I sat alone (returns to chair and sits), the angel Gabriel appeared.

GABRIEL *(entering):* The Lord be with you, Mary. You are most favored among women. *(As Mary looks up at him, startled or afraid)* Do not be afraid, Mary. God has looked with favor upon you. You will conceive and bear a Son, who shall be named Jesus. He will be great, for He will be called the Son of the Most High. The Lord God will give Him the throne of His ancestor, King David, for He will indeed be King over Israel forever. His reign shall never end.

MARY *(in wonderment):* How can this be when I am not married?

GABRIEL: The Holy Spirit will come upon you, and the power
    of the Most High will overshadow you. This is why that
    holy child will be called the Son of God.
MARY *(humbly):* Here I am. I am the Lord's handmaid. Let it
    be as you have told me.

(Gabriel leaves, and Mary sits with head bowed for a moment. Spotlight goes out and there is a musical interlude of a few lines of "Fairest Lord Jesus." Then Mary stands and comes to front of stage, and the spotlight comes on.)

MARY: Even so, it was difficult. I almost couldn't believe what
    I saw and heard. So many thoughts and questions went
    through my mind. For days it was like this. What would
    Joseph think? Would he believe me? What about our
    neighbors and friends in Nazareth when they learned? It
    would be such a long time before I would be free to speak.
    It was too awesome a thing to speak of. Then I remem-
    bered that the angel mentioned Elisabeth, that she also
    was expecting a child. I decided to visit her. *(Leaves stage
    accompanied by soft background music. Reenters with
    Elisabeth, and they stand in spotlight focused there.)* I have
    so much to tell you, Elisabeth.
ELISABETH: God has blessed us both, but you above all
    women. His blessing is also on the child you bear. Who am
    I, that the mother of my Lord should visit me? When I
    heard your greeting, my own child moved within me. How
    happy and blessed is she who has had such faith in the
    Lord's promise that in her it will be fulfilled!

(Mary's song of thanksgiving [Magnificat] may be sung by Mary or another person as Mary and Elisabeth stand together. Then spotlight goes off and they leave. Joseph enters and paces back and forth across front of stage.)

JOSEPH: What shall I do? According to our law Mary should
    be stoned, but I can never do that. How can I save her from
    public disgrace? Perhaps a quiet, private divorce would be
    best. *(Sinks down on the chair, and seems to doze off with
    head in hands. There may be soft background music.)*
GABRIEL *(entering):* Joseph, son of David, do not be afraid. Do
    not fear to bring Mary home as your wife. The child she is
    carrying is conceived through the Holy Spirit. She will

bear a Son, and you shall call His name Jesus, for He shall save His people from their sins.

(Joseph rises and leaves opposite Mary's entrance. Mary enters and sits down. Choir, Chorus, or instrument provides music: "It Came Upon the Midnight Clear." Afterward, Luke comes forward to address Mary.)

LUKE: You and Joseph were married, then?
MARY: Yes. We came here to our home, but did not live as husband and wife until my Son was born.
LUKE: What happened next?
MARY: In those days, Emperor Augustus issued a decree for a general registration, for a taxation. Cyrenius was then governor of Syria. And so Joseph and I went up to Judaea to the town of Bethlehem, because we both were descended from David. It was a long, tiring journey, at least a hundred miles, and I knew that my baby would be born soon.

(As Mary speaks, Joseph reenters and they move to the exit where the spotlight is focused. Choir, Chorus, or instrument provides music: "O Little Town of Bethlehem." Afterward Joseph knocks and Innkeeper looks out on stage.)

JOSEPH: I would like a room for my wife and myself.
INNKEEPER *(opening door wider)*: Room? You must be joking! Our town is overcrowded because of the census. I have no vacancy.
INNKEEPER'S WIFE *(joining Innkeeper and looking out)*: What is it? Who's there? *(Seeing Mary)* You must be very tired. How far have you traveled?
MARY: From Nazareth.
INNKEEPER'S WIFE *(to Innkeeper)*: I know what you are going to say. We have no room. But we must do something for these two.
INNKEEPER: What can we do? Even our own room is rented.
JOSEPH *(taking Mary's arm and turning as if to go)*: It is all right. We understand. We will look elsewhere.
INNKEEPER'S WIFE: I'm sure you won't find a place this late, and you shouldn't be traveling in your condition!
INNKEEPER: Wait a minute. What about a place in back?
INNKEEPER'S WIFE: What place? There's nothing back there but—

INNKEEPER: Well, it is clean, and it is a shelter. It is better than nothing.

(Joseph and Mary move back toward center stage and Innkeeper closes door. Choir, Chorus, or instrument provides music: "What Child Is This?" This may be a solo accompanied by a guitar. Afterward Joseph leaves, Mary sits, and Luke goes to her.)

LUKE: You had to stay in the stable then?
MARY: Yes, during that busy time of the census. While we were there Jesus was born. I wrapped Him in some soft cloths and laid Him in a manger. It was a beautiful night, a holy night.
LUKE: Did anyone else know?
MARY: Yes, but we didn't know it right away. A little later some shepherds came.

(Spotlight the area on shepherd scene. Choir, Chorus, or instrument provides music: "While Shepherds Watched Their Flocks.")

FIRST SHEPHERD *(scanning area)*: Does the sky seem brighter tonight?
SECOND SHEPHERD *(yawning)*: I hadn't noticed.
THIRD SHEPHERD: There are many stars out tonight. *(Looking up)* On such nights they seem to hang lower over the earth.

(Show spotlight.)

FIRST SHEPHERD *(frightened)*: But that is no starlight!

(They all show fright as Gabriel enters and stands in spotlight.)

GABRIEL: Do not be afraid, for I bring good news. There will be great joy among all people. For in the city of David a Savior has been born this day, and He is Messiah, the Lord. And this shall be a sign to you: you will find a newborn child wrapped in swaddling clothes and lying in a manger.

(Other Angels join Gabriel. If these are a Choir, they sing the third stanza and chorus of "Angels We Have Heard on High." If they are to speak, the lines are given below.)

ANGEL VOICES: Glory to God in the highest!

ANGEL VOICES: And on earth may there be peace.

ANGEL VOICES: May there be peace and goodwill among
men on whom the favor of the Lord rests.

(Gabriel and Angels leave spotlight area.)

SECOND SHEPHERD: Come, let us go to Bethlehem at once.

THIRD SHEPHERD: Let us see this thing that has happened,
as the Lord has told us.

*(Shepherds move to center stage and kneel. Mary moves to
the front of stage into the spotlight with Luke.)*

MARY: The shepherds told us what the angel said. Everyone
was surprised, but I remembered their words and thought
them over many times since.

*(Shepherds leave. Mary and Luke return to center stage in
spotlight.)*

LUKE: Were there others who came to see Jesus?

MARY: At the time Jesus was born in Bethlehem, Herod was
king. Wise-men came from the East seeking a King, so
they came first to Jerusalem.

*(Spotlight off center stage and on at the exit. The Wise-men
enter, followed by Herod and Chief Priest. Choir, Chorus, or
instrument provides music: "We Three Kings of Orient Are.")*

FIRST WISE-MAN: Where is the child who has been born the
King of the Jews?

SECOND WISE-MAN: In the East we saw His star.

THIRD WISE-MAN: We have come a great distance to see Him
and to worship Him.

CHIEF PRIEST: In Bethlehem of Judea, as the prophet Micah
has written: "Bethlehem, in the land of Judah, you are not
the least among the rulers of Judah; for from you shall
come the one who is to be the Shepherd of my people Israel."

(Chief Priest leaves and Herod turns to speak to Wise-men.)

HEROD: Go, then, and make a careful inquiry concerning this
child. When you have found Him, return to me, so that I
may go to Him myself and pay Him honor.

(Herod leaves and Wise-men go to center stage and kneel. Spotlight on Mary and Small Child. Luke moves forward.)

LUKE: Then Herod came and worshiped Him too?

MARY: Oh, no; the Wise-men were warned in a dream not to return to Herod. They went home another way.

(Wise-men and Child leave as Luke and Mary continue.)

LUKE: It is unusual to disobey a king. How did he take that?

MARY: After the Wise-men had gone away, an angel of the Lord appeared to Joseph in a dream. He told Joseph to take us to Egypt, to stay there until further word. This was because Herod intended to find the child and do away with Him.

LUKE: And Herod?

MARY: I understand that he was so angry he was not to be outdone. Having no information except the time when the star appeared to the Wise-men, he set about to destroy all infants in Bethlehem up to two years old. *(Shudders.)* Such a tragedy, and, of course useless, for we were safe in Egypt. After a while Herod died and the angel spoke again to Joseph, telling him to bring us back to the land of Israel.

LUKE: Did Herod have a son to inherit the throne?

MARY: Yes, and Archelaus was his name. Joseph was afraid to go there, but again an angel guided him, and we came back to Galilee and settled in Nazareth. This fulfilled the words of the prophet: "He shall be called a Nazarene."

(All lights come on, and the youth come on stage. Others resume positions held at the beginning.)

DIRECTOR: That is it. What do you think?

YOUTH 5: Well, it's the same story all right, but somehow it was different.

YOUTH 2: I thought it was more realistic.

YOUTH 3: I began to think about what it was like to have been there.

DIRECTOR: Good! Anything else?

YOUTH 4: To me it was really Christmas—not like today.

YOUTH 5: Why not?

YOUTH 4: Well, like they say—it's so commercial.

DIRECTOR: Whose fault is that?

YOUTH 6: The stores, advertisers—
YOUTH 1: I don't agree. Christmas hasn't changed, only people have changed the meaning.
YOUTH 3: Christmas should really be the best and easiest time to tell people about Jesus.
YOUTH 1: Just about everyone celebrates His birth, but a lot of people don't even know why.
YOUTH 2: Yeah; how many times at Christmas do you hear people explaining that God loves us so much He sent His Son to be crucified, to save sinners like us. That is what the Christmas story is all about.
YOUTH 5: Everybody's always so busy at Christmas there isn't much talk about the meaning—except in church.
DIRECTOR: How can that be changed?
YOUTH 3: You start with yourself—
DIRECTOR: Good! That is right. Also, talk with your parents. If we become more aware of the real meaning of Christmas, we'll be able to express it to others easier.

(Choir, Chorus, or recording provides music: "Joy to the World"; softly sung or played.)

YOUTH 5: Oh, some carolers are coming!
YOUTH 4: Let's go out and listen.

(Characters onstage come to front, facing audience. Choir rises if it occupies a loft or balcony, but joins the others onstage if it is in the back, singing as it moves down the aisle.)

YOUTH 6: Don't forget to invite them to the play!

(All participants stand and join in singing "Joy to the World.")

A Present-day Play

Roadside Christmas

Rebecca McTavish

Cast: Ted Wells
Alice Wells, his wife
Jackie Wells, their daughter, a teen
Mrs. Sloan
Miss Smith
Chauffeur
Mrs. Lane
Margie Lane, her daughter, about ten
Tony Lane, about twelve
Truck Driver

(NOTE: Jackie Wells should be able to play a guitar or piano, and sing.)

SCENE I

Setting: During the first scene the stage is dark. The first dialogue is spoken offstage, with microphones if available. There are also certain sound effects necessary.

TED: Wow! This is a terrible snowstorm. The road is slick.
ALICE *(fearfully):* Maybe we ought to pull over for the night. This is making me so nervous, riding along, practically blind, on a sheet of ice!
JACKIE: But, Mom, we *have* to get to Grandma's tonight. It's Christmas Eve! We just have to keep going!
ALICE: It's more important to be in one piece, Jackie.

(There is the sound of brakes squealing, along with crashing and banging, and some screams. After that, silence.)

TED *(in shaky voice):* Is—Is everyone O.K.? Alice? Jackie?

JACKIE (*weakly*): Yeah, Dad. I—I think I'm O.K.

TED: Alice, what about you? Are you hurt?

ALICE: I'm not hurt, I'm—I'm fine, just a little scared. But, Ted, what's that? (*Voice rises*) We're stuck in a snowdrift. We'll *never* be able to get out without help. Just look at this!

TED (*soothingly, trying to be calm*): I know, I know, Alice. But it doesn't matter, since we are all still alive and unhurt.

ALICE (*more calmly*): Whew! I know God is always with us, no matter what happens, but I still can't seem to stop shaking.

TED: Well, let us just calm down and get our bearings.

JACKIE (*after a pause*): Look, Mom, Dad! There's a light just over there. Looks like it might be a restaurant or gas station. Let's go over there. Maybe they can help us!

TED: Good idea, Jackie. Now, why don't you try to open your door? I can't get out on my side because of the snowdrift.

JACKIE: O.K., Dad. (*Sound of car door opening and shutting.*)

SCENE II

Setting: Inside a restaurant. There should be enough tables and chairs and perhaps a counter, to look like a diner.

(*As scene opens, Mrs. Sloan may be wiping off counter or a table. After a few minutes Ted, Alice, and Jackie enter, dressed in heavy outdoor clothing, shivering and stomping their feet. They may ad lib comments about the cold and the storm.*)

MRS. SLOAN (*looking up as they enter*): Sorry, folks, but I'm just closin'. Christmas Eve, you know.

TED (*apologetically*): Ma'am, I am Ted Wells, and this is my wife, Alice, and our daughter, Jackie. Our car just slid off the road into a snowbank, and we'll need some help. Is there someone to call who could do something?

MRS. SLOAN (*sighing*): Oh, boy! Don't know anybody who could this late, it being Christmas Eve. State road crew always comes through to clean the road after a storm at night, but probably won't be through till mornin'— 'course, it being Christmas, we can't even be sure of that, in this case.

TED: Well, then, is there a motel around here?

MRS. SLOAN: Hmmph! You folks are right in the heart of Crossroads, Minnesota, at least fifteen miles from anywhere. The only place you're gonna be able to bed down for the night is here on the floor or out in a snowdrift.

ALICE *(anxiously and timidly):* Would it be all right, then, if we did stay here?

MRS. SLOAN: To be honest with you, I was countin' on goin' home now, but if the roads are as bad as that, I guess there's no point in tryin' to go anywhere. My husband's a trucker, and not due in till tomorrow afternoon, so it's not like anybody's waitin' for me at home. So we all might just as well wait out the storm here together.

ALICE: That's really kind of you—to let us stay here, I mean. What did you say your name was?

MRS. SLOAN: Didn't say, but it's Nell—Nell Sloan.

(As she finishes speaking the door blows open and Miss Smith and Chauffeur enter. She strides in angrily and he follows.)

MISS SMITH: You idiot! Only a simpleton would drive a brand new Cadillac into a snowdrift!

CHAUFFEUR: I'm truly sorry, Ma'am. There was nothing I could do. The road was too slick!

MISS SMITH: Well, whatever must be done, I must get to Minneapolis tonight. *(Suddenly she turns to Ted and points her finger at him.)* You! You call me a cab, immediately!

MRS. SLOAN *(laughing loudly, looking up at ceiling and holding up both hands):* I don't believe this! I just don't believe it! Why didn't I have sense enough to go home an hour early tonight? Why me? *(Turning to Miss Smith, who has calmed down and is looking at her)* Lady, there's no way you're gonna get to Minneapolis—or anyplace else—tonight, just no way. You might as well sit down and relax.

MISS SMITH *(stamping her foot):* No, no! It can't be! I must get to Minneapolis, and that is that!

MRS. SLOAN: Well, I'd think twice about that if I was you. The only way is to hoof it, and it's a long walk.

MISS SMITH *(shocked):* Well, no one *ever* talked to me that way before, never! *(Haughtily)* Do you have any idea to whom you are speaking?

MRS. SLOAN: I have no idea, but I could care less. Look, lady, like it or not, you're stuck here, so you might as well cool it. *(More gently)* Now, look. Do you think the rest of us are waitin' around here because we *want* to?

MISS SMITH: Well, I never— *(Sits down, looking at Mrs. Sloan with disgust.)*

(Everyone stands or sits, talking in low tones, except for Miss Smith, who is silent. Trucker enters.)

TRUCKER *(entering hurriedly and slamming door):* What a night! Hey, got a phone in this joint? My rig just went clear off the road, and I'm gonna need help to pull it out. Tried to call for help on the CB, but I couldn't get a rise out of nobody!

(Some of the others chuckle, and ad lib remarks.)

JACKIE: Mister, join the club. You've got the same problem that everybody else has.

TRUCKER: What d'ya mean?

MISS SMITH *(indignantly):* She simply means that, just as the rest of us, you have the desire to be going somewhere, but not the ability! This place is ill-equipped, to say the least. No working phone, no tow trucks, *nothing!*

TRUCKER: Y'don't say! I was supposed to make it home tonight. It's Christmas Eve, y'know. My wife and kids are expecting me. *(Speaking angrily as he paces the floor)* I've *got* to get out of here!

TED: In this storm, with everyone skidding on and off the roads? You might as well calm down, because you're stuck here like the rest of us.

TRUCKER *(disgusted):* Calm down? Stuck in the middle of nowhere, and who knows how long? This is a crummy excuse for the Christmas Eve!

ALICE: Well, we know how you feel. At least you're not alone. *(She tries to be consoling. He looks at her strangely without answering, but sighs, turns away, and sit down near Chauffeur.)*

MRS. SLOAN: Boy, what did I ever do to deserve all of you? Spending Christmas Eve with such a bunch of soreheads. *(Shakes head.)*

(Voices are heard offstage.)

CHAUFFEUR: More company!

MRS. SLOAN: Oh, no. Not more people! This place is turning into Grand Central Station!

(Mrs. Lane, Margie, and Tony enter, stamping and shivering.)

TONY: Look at all the other people here, Mom!

MRS. LANE *(tired and sad):* Oh, my, but it's cold out there! Our car skidded and got stuck. It seems we have walked for miles and miles. *(Turning to Margie)* Oh, sweetie, are you all right?

MARGIE *(taking off her coat):* I'm O.K., Mom, just tired and my feet are cold—and, well, maybe I'm a little hungry. *(Looks at Mrs. Lane shyly.)*

TONY: Oh, you're not hungry, Margie. You just ate a big meal at suppertime.

MRS. SLOAN *(having listened carefully):* Seems to me all three of you could use somethin' to stick to your ribs, especially after trudgin' through the snow like you did.

MRS. LANE: No, really, we're all right. We'll just wait here till a snowplow comes through, if it's all right with you.

MRS. SLOAN: Sure, you can stay here. That's what everybody else is doin'—just waitin'.

TED *(to Mrs. Lane):* But, lady, you may be here for a while, maybe until tomorrow. You better go ahead and get some food.

MRS. LANE *(looking stricken):* Oh, no! You don't mean it! What are we going to do? *(Buries her face in her hands and plops down in a chair.)*

ALICE *(going to comfort Mrs. Lane):* It's going to be all right. Don't worry, please don't.

(As Alice speaks, Tony and Margie go to her. Margie kneels at her feet, leaning against her knee, and begins to cry softly. Tony stands behind Margie, with his hand on her shoulder.)

TONY: She's right, Mom. We'll all be O.K., I know we will. *(To Alice)* You see, our dad just died, and we're on our way to St. Paul to live with our grandmother. But we don't have much money, and that's why Mom is upset.

MRS. SLOAN *(overhearing):* Well, for land sakes! Don't fret about that. A rich lady pulled in a while ago, and is treatin' everybody tonight!

(At that last remark, Miss Smith opens her mouth as if to protest, but closes it again and remains silent.)

MARGIE *(looking toward Miss Smith as Mrs. Sloan speaks):* Thank you, lady. That's awfully nice of you.

(Miss Smith smiles weakly and insincerely, and nods.)

MRS. SLOAN: Think I'll go into that kitchen and whip up a batch of sandwiches, and put on some hot chocolate. That should cheer everybody up a bit. Besides, it's sure better to be in there cookin' than lookin' at some of you. *(Directs last remark toward Miss Smith, who greets it with an equally cold look, and leaves.)*

ALICE *(to Mrs. Lane):* Let's go into the kitchen too, and get a cup of coffee for you. You children, why don't you stay out here? We'll have something for you in just a few minutes. *(Helps Mrs. Lane offstage, as children look after them, looking sad and huddling together.)*

JACKIE: You know, Dad, everybody *does* look pretty sad and pitiful, just like Mrs. Sloan said. Maybe if it were more Christmasy looking in here, people would feel better. What do you think?

TED: Maybe you're right. Why don't you go over and talk to those kids? You might be able to come up with some ideas.

JACKIE *(going to the Lane children):* Hi! I'm Jackie Wells. That man over there *(pointing to Ted)* is my dad, and that lady who just went into the kitchen with your mother is my mom. We were going to visit my grandmother, just like you were going to see yours, but it doesn't look like we'll be getting there real soon either.

TONY *(discouraged):* It doesn't look too good, does it? I'm Tony Lane, and this is my sister, Margie. We really need to get to our grandmother's soon.

JACKIE: Well, I know everything will be all right. Everything will be for the best. Just believe in God, that He will take care of all your needs. He knows you need help right now.

TONY *(surprised):* Why, that's just what my Sunday-school teacher says. Do you really believe that?

JACKIE: I sure do, and my parents do too. I just have to believe that there is always a reason for everything that happens, and instead of getting all upset about it, it's just better to accept it and make the best of the situation.

MARGIE *(interested):* Well, how can we make the best of this?

JACKIE: Well, I was just thinking. If only it looked more like Christmas in here—

MARGIE: If only we had a tree!

TONY: Hey, that's an idea—But how are we going to get one?

JACKIE *(with enthusiasm):* Maybe the lady who owns this place would have an axe. There are lots of evergreen trees around here. Maybe my dad would help us.

TED: I heard that, kids, and I've got an axe in the car. I'll go out and get it, and see if I can find a tree close by. While I'm gone, maybe you can find some decorations.

TRUCKER *(standing up and going to Ted):* Hey, I'll go with you. It's better than sittin' around here feelin' sorry for myself. I've got two boys at home just about the size of those kids. If I can't be with my own kids on Christmas Eve, I can help them make the most of it.

TED *(smiling):* Come ahead. Glad to have some company!

CHAUFFEUR: Wait for me. I'll go too.

MISS SMITH: What? You wouldn't dare leave me alone here in this—this hovel!

CHAUFFEUR *(with authority):* Oh, sit down and be quiet. Nobody's leavin' nobody, and nothing's going to happen to you. Frettin' won't make the storm stop any sooner.

MISS SMITH: Sometimes I wonder why I don't fire you!

CHAUFFEUR *(sweetly):* Maybe it's because you couldn't find anybody else willing to take the job.

(The three men leave. During all this, the children are quietly huddled together, still frightened.)

MARGIE *(going over to Miss Smith):* Don't worry, lady. He'll be back. Maybe if you'd just be a little nicer to him, and more patient, he'd like you better, and you could get along with each other without yelling. My mother always says that the best way to get along is to do to others the same way we would have them do to us. It's kinda hard for Tony and me, but we try.

MISS SMITH *(totally surprised):* Hmmph! So you believe that?

MARGIE: Yes. Even though it's hard, it is worse to be yelling at each other. It's more fun to be friends, and like Tony and me, we share and do favors for each other, and it's really neat.

TONY (*who has been talking in whispers with Jackie*): Hey, Margie, maybe the lady would have some cranberries or some popcorn. We could string that for the tree.

MARGIE: That would really make it pretty. Let's go ask her. (*Turning back to Miss Smith*) Got to go now to find some decorations.

(*Pats her on the knee, and joins the others. They leave, ad libbing comments about the decorations: "We can make some pretty ones," or "That's a great idea." After a pause, the men reenter with a tree, making a lot of noise and comments about handling it and where to put it.*)

TRUCKER: Well, men, this is a beauty.

CHAUFFEUR: It didn't take long to find, either. Not far from the road, almost like it was sitting out there just asking to be cut for a Christmas tree.

TED: Maybe it was. Hey, kids! (*Calling toward "kitchen"*) We've got a tree!

(*Children rush in, carrying strings of cranberries and popcorn.*)

MARGIE: Oh, isn't it pretty?

TED: And look, it's even got a stand.

TONY: Wow! Where did the stand come from? It didn't grow that way, did it?

TRUCKER (*chuckling*): That sounds like something a kid from the city would ask. I had the stand in my truck, and it sure came in handy.

JACKIE: C'mon! Let's decorate it!

(*They all help with the tree, then Mrs. Sloan enters with a tray of sandwiches and hot chocolate. Alice follows carrying candles, and Mrs. Lane carries a tray of dishes.*)

MRS. SLOAN: All right, everyone. Come and get some hot chocolate and sandwiches.

(*Everyone except Miss Smith goes to table or counter to help himself. Margie picks up two cups and goes to Miss Smith.*)

MARGIE: Won't you have some hot chocolate? (*Tasting her own*) It tastes real good! (*Settles herself at Miss Smith's feet.*)

(While the others are serving themselves, settling down, and eating, Alice places the candles around the room and lights them. As she completes this, the other stage lights are dimmed.)

ALICE: There! Now it looks more like Christmas in here. Now, I think it would be a good idea for us to sing for our supper—when we have finished. Jackie can play her guitar, and we can sing along with her. Whenever you are ready, Jackie.

JACKIE *(settling with guitar)*: Sure, Mom. *(She strums a few songs, playing and singing until the others are through eating.)* What carol would you like to sing first?

MARGIE: "O Little Town of Bethlehem."

(Follow with a few other suggestions from the others, singing a stanza or two of each.)

MISS SMITH *(when singing is over)*: You, John, will you go out to the car and bring in my overnight bag? It's on the back seat.

CHAUFFEUR: Oh, no, Miss Smith, you're not serious.

MISS SMITH *(looking down at Margie who looks up at her)*: I know it is cold and snowy out there, John *(speaking very politely)*, but I would appreciate it if you would please get it for me.

CHAUFFEUR *(sighing)*: Well, I guess so. *(Puts on coat and leaves.)*

(Margie smiles at Miss Smith, who looks back a little puzzled, then smiles back.)

TED *(reaching into his suit pocket)*: I have my New Testament with me. Don't you think that it would be a good time, when John comes back, to read the Christmas story? We could sing "Silent Night" first.

(Sounds of approval, and Jackie begins carol. Chauffeur returns during singing and puts the bag beside Miss Smith's chair.)

MISS SMITH *(after the singing)*: Thank you very much, John.

CHAUFFEUR *(surprised)*: You're welcome!

JACKIE: I think we're ready for the Christmas story now, Dad.

(Ted stands and reads Luke 2:1-20 from a pocket Testament.)

ALICE: I think the Christmas story is so beautiful.

JACKIE: When Jesus was born on that night in Bethlehem, His parents were a long way from home too.

MARGIE: We learned the story in church, how the baby Jesus was born in a manger. *(Turning to Mrs. Lane.)* See, Mom? We have it nicer tonight than even Jesus did when He was born.

MRS. LANE *(nodding and smiling):* You're right, Margie. We tend to approach Christmas with certain ideas of what it ought to be like, but those things do not necessarily make Christmas what it really is.

ALICE: Yes, that is right. Even though the storm is unfortunate, God still has taken care of us tonight. What could we ask for? We are all warm and fed, and we have the fellowship of other travelers, friends whom we would perhaps never have met otherwise. What a blessing!

MISS SMITH *(who has been writing):* Yes, it *is* a blessing! *(Everyone else turns toward her, surprised.)* I learned something special tonight about human nature, and I learned this from a little girl. Because it's Christmas, the time for giving gifts, I'd like to give something to all the young folk here. *(Handing checks to Mrs. Lane and Ted, who are hesitant).* Please take them and use them for something for your children. And because Margie gave me something special, I'd like to give her something in return. *(Offers Margie a necklace from a small jewelry box.)* This is for you, Margie.

MARGIE *(surprised):* Oh, no! I didn't do anything.

MISS SMITH: Oh, yes, you did. *(Fastening it around Margie's neck)* You were kind to me, and gave me some valuable advice that I had known once but had long forgotten. When you wear this, perhaps you will remember me, for I will not forget you.

MARGIE: Thank you! It's beautiful. Look, Mommy, Tony! *(Shows it off to the others who ad lib comments, "Yes," "It really is," or "Isn't it lovely?" and nod approvingly.)*

MRS. SLOAN *(wiping eyes):* Love is what Christmas is all about, and so many times we say things that are hateful, and hurt other people when we don't even think what we're doin'! *(To Miss Smith)* I guess I had you pegged all wrong, Ma'am. You got a heart in you same as anybody else. I'm sorry if I was rude to you.

MISS SMITH *(kindly):* Well, the way I acted, I probably got what I deserved.

TED: Well, no one's perfect, but God loves us anyway. That is why He sent His Son, so that if we believe in Him He will forgive our sins. If we try to live the kind of life He wants us to live and obey Him, He will help us.

ALICE: He can turn us all into loving, caring people, if we just let Him.

JACKIE: There's a song, "I'll Go Where You Want Me to Go," and what Mom said reminded me of it. The words go like this. *(Sings "I'll Go Where You Want Me to Go," accompanied by the guitar.)* If you think you can follow along, join me in the chorus. *(Repeats chorus, others joining in.)*

TONY: That's a neat song. Wonder what God wants us to do?

TED: Maybe right now He just wants us to be patient and wait for the storm to end. In the meantime He's given us time to get acquainted with each other, given us a chance to meet people we might never have met. And, too, I think He has shown us that there are other ways to celebrate the birth of His Son than just the ways we each planned.

MARGIE: You know what? That's a Christmas present—a wonderful Christmas present.

MRS. LANE: What is, Margie?

MARGIE: Our new friends—lots of new friends.

MISS SMITH: How right you are!

(Sound effect of a truck offstage.)

TONY *(looking out):* Hey! It's stopped snowing, and the snowplow is here.

TRUCKER: That means the salt trucks will be out too.

MARGIE: Oh, then everybody can go on. We might get to Grandma's in time for Christmas dinner. Hey, everybody *(begins to sing)* "I Wish You a Merry Christmas."

(Stage lights come on. Everyone else joins in singing "We Wish You a Merry Christmas." They wave to audience and call "Merry Christmas" as they begin to leave.)

(Curtain)

No Room in the Inn

Doris Faulkner

Participants: Innkeeper's Wife
Mary
Joseph
Shepherds
Angel
Wise-men
Choir or Chorus

(NOTE: The Innkeeper's Wife has the only speaking part. The Bible characters pantomime, and the Choir or Chorus provides the background for the action. Choir may be seen or unseen.)

Staging: The pantomime will be most effective if it is presented with broader gestures than those that usually accompany dialogue. If a fire is desired for the shepherd scene, use a tray containing a lighted flashlight, over which is placed a few sticks. This can be placed at the appropriate time and then removed easily. If there is to be no curtain, the stage may be darkened, and during this scene a folding screen may be placed to conceal the stable. Entrances may be from backstage or aisle of auditorium.

Properties: An oil lamp or candle, a flask of water, narrow strips of white cloth, a blanket or two, and fancy boxes and a pretty bottle or vase. For candlelight service, small candles should be available for the audience.

Costumes: Traditional costumes for those in pantomime. Wise-men should be arrayed as elaborately as possible. Choir may wear robes if Choir is to be seen.

SCENE I

Setting: The courtyard of the inn. One side of stage is set up as the stable. At the other side is the door to the inn.

PRELUDE: A medley of carols not used in the drama
CHOIR: "Thou Didst Leave Thy Throne" (stanzas 1 and 2)
PANTOMIME: Mary and Joseph enter slowly from side entrance or the aisle, Joseph supporting Mary. They go to door of the inn and Joseph knocks. Door opens and Innkeeper's Wife pantomimes "no room." She begins to close door, then opens it wider, looking more intently at Mary. She signals to wait and goes inside the inn, leaving door open. During these moments, Joseph is comforting Mary. Innkeeper's Wife returns with blanket and the oil lamp or candle. She escorts them to the stable and spreads the blanket. She and Joseph assist Mary to a seat on the blanket. She pantomimes her understanding of Mary's plight, placing her hand on Mary's shoulder. She looks about as if to be thinking what else she can do to help. Signaling them to wait, she hurries back to inn. Joseph offers Mary a drink of water from the flask, or smooths blanket for her. Innkeeper's Wife returns with the strips of cloth (swaddling clothes), unrolling a portion of it to show Mary. Pointing to herself and making a cradle of her arms, she shakes her head sorrowfully and gives the cloths to Mary, who graciously accepts them. These actions should indicate that these might have belonged to a baby that the Innkeeper's Wife had lost, or perhaps to a child she had hoped for but never had.

(If the pantomime is not completed with the end of the Choir number, the song could be played softly and the Choir hum until the Innkeeper's Wife has presented the cloths to Mary. The music should stop by the time she crosses the courtyard to a spot at the inn door, where she speaks.)

INNKEEPER'S WIFE: "No room!" I said to them, and would have shut the door. The inn was overcrowded and I was bone-tired. I had been up since dawn. But then I saw that the young woman was great with child. She spoke no word, but anyone could see that her time was near. Could I then refuse her shelter in her hour of need? But where? I had given up my own space for other latecomers. Then I recalled the stable, where at least she would have some warmth and privacy and they would have shelter. With just a small lamp to light the way, we crossed the courtyard to the cattle stall, and there, with no more comfort than a bed of straw, I left them to rest. *(Leaves through inn door.)*

(Curtain or stage is darkened)

CHOIR: "There's a Song in the Air"

SCENE II

Setting: A Judean hillside. The folding screen should be placed to conceal the stable. Dim light on the scene.

CHOIR: "Winds Through the Olive Trees" or "O Little Town of Bethlehem"

PANTOMIME: Shepherds are seated or reclining near fire, and perhaps one or two are standing on guard. One may rub his hands together over fire, another may pull his shawl about him. Those around the fire may settle down, covering themselves with blankets. When the carol is finished, there is a short pause, then a bright spotlight shines down upon the Shepherds as the Angel enters.

CHOIR: "While Shepherds Watched Their Flocks by Night" (first four stanzas)

PANTOMIME: Shepherds sit up, rub their eyes, suiting the pantomime to the carol, showing fright and then wonder in their actions. Angel appears to be telling the message.

CHOIR: "Angels We Have Heard on High" (chorus only)

PANTOMIME: Shepherds hold positions, listening to the angel chorus in awe and wonder. At the end of the chorus Angel leaves and spotlight goes off. Shepherds then pantomime the words of the Scripture, "Let us go to Bethlehem and see," etc. One may bring a blanket and another a lamb, suggestive as gifts for the Christ child. They hurry offstage, reentering from the rear of auditorium to foot of the stage.

(In order for the Shepherds to exit and reenter, the Choir may sing the chorus as many as three times, with an upward

key change each time; or they may sing "Hark, the Herald Angels Sing.")

(Curtain or stage is darkened)

SCENE III

Setting: The courtyard, same as Scene I. Remove folding screen. Mary is seated beside manger and Joseph stands near her. As both gaze down into the manger their faces are illumined by a light shining from the manger.

CHOIR: "What Child Is This?" or "O Come, All Ye Faithful"
PANTOMIME: Shepherds leave foot of stage and enter stage at appropriate time in song. They go to stable and kneel at the manger. They present their gifts, then all hold their positions during next song.
CHOIR: "Silent Night," "O Holy Night," or "Once in Royal David's City"

(Curtain or stage is darkened)

SCENE IV

Setting: The same, but screen is replaced.

(There may be an instrumental interlude to indicate the passage of time. A star may appear overhead at this time.)

CHOIR: "We Three Kings of Orient Are"
PANTOMIME: The Wise-men come down the aisle of auditorium, marching majestically. If the first stanza and chorus of song are not long enough for them to reach the foot of the stage, there may be an introduction before the words are begun. Each Wise-man may sing his own stanza as he mounts the stage and approaches the child, now held by Joseph with Mary standing by (no manger). But the words for each Wise-man could be male solos in the Choir. Tableau may remain during song, with the Shepherds joining, or participants may withdraw, if this is final scene.
CHOIR: "Joy to the World"

(Curtain or stage is darkened)

EPILOGUE

Setting: The courtyard, as in Scene I. Stable is seen, but there are no occupants. The lamp is still there and still burning. The Innkeeper's Wife enters from door of inn, and goes to stable, looking at the empty manger, and all around her, as if remembering all the things she has seen and heard. Then she returns to inn door to speak.

INNKEEPER'S WIFE: They have gone. After the census the couple found lodging in a house, but since have gone on to Egypt. So once again this stable is just a place to shelter the sheep and cattle from the cold. Yet, how can one forget? Here in this lowly stall a King was born, with nothing but a manger for His bed. Will this be remembered, years from now? How will it be remembered? Will people view the innkeeper in scorn, even though the inn was crowded? I thought to turn the child away, that is true; And yet I found a place for Him. Have you? *(She leaves through inn door.)*

SOLO or CONGREGATION: "O Little Town of Bethlehem" (last stanza)

PRAYER THOUGHTS *(for minister or leader):* As we view the stable on this occasion, we acknowledge that we have not always found a place for God's only begotten Son. Often we have been caught up in the routine of living, and so there has been scant room for Jesus in our hearts. Sometimes we have been so distracted by the pleasures of the world that we have been unmindful of the blessedness of God's Gift to the world, given to us in the birth of the Savior. May we have uncluttered hearts that will open wide to make room for the Christ child. As we light our candles from the lamp in the stable, let us remember that Jesus is the light of the world, and that we would be in utter darkness if it had not been for the miracle of His birth.

SONG *(by congregation):* "O Come, All Ye Faithful"

(The minister or leader lights a candle from the lamp in the stable and lights those of two ushers. They in turn ignite those of the first person at the end of the aisles. They each pass the light along to the people in their rows, until the auditorium is illuminated. This may be done to a medley of hymns concerning light, especially Jesus as the light of the world.)

Christmas Gifts

Florence Harper Haney

Cast: Carolyn Price
Brad, her husband
Russ, their son
Cindy, their daughter
Faye, Carolyn's sister
Joan, Russ's girl friend
Kent, Cindy's boyfriend
Donna, Joan's little sister
Bobby, their brother

SCENE I

Time: Sometime before Christmas.
Place: The Price living room.
Setting: Furnishings should include a folding table. There should be two exits, one for the "outside" and the other for the "kitchen."

(As curtain opens, Carolyn is seated at the folding table, sorting through lists and file cards, pen or pencil in hand, now and then sipping from a cup of coffee.)

CAROLYN *(to herself):* Christmas cards addressed and stamped, check. Turkey ordered, check. Tie bought and wrapped for Uncle Walt, check. *(She checks each item with a flourish; then there is a knock at door.)* Who could that be? I don't have time for interruptions. I have too much to do. *(Goes to door and steps back as Faye enters with bulging shopping bag.)*

FAYE: I will not go down to that shopping center again, Carolyn! Not ever again! *(Drops into chair.)*

CAROLYN *(sitting back down to resume her work):* Well,

Merry Christmas to you too, Faye. What's the matter now?

FAYE: I've had it, that's all! I tell you, Christmas is just not worth all this hassle! Every year it gets worse.

CAROLYN *(not really listening):* Stores crowded, I suppose?

FAYE: Those people aren't crowds! That's a mob out there! How can the minister preach about peace and goodwill among men? It's more like push and shove among shoppers out there.

CAROLYN: Well, you know it is like this every year. Why do you wait till the last minute? I did most of my shopping back in July during the sales. I've just been checking my lists, and—

FAYE: Don't be so smug, Carolyn. Can't stand a smug sister. I just stopped here for a quick cup of coffee—before I have to face another madhouse at home.

CAROLYN: From mob to madhouse. Sounds like real fun. The coffee's in the kitchen; help yourself.

(Faye leaves as Carolyn continues checking her lists, humming a carol. Faye returns with cup, sits down, sighing deeply.)

FAYE: Ah, that helps.

CAROLYN: You know, Faye, if you would just get organized—

FAYE: Don't preach at me, Carolyn. You do things your way, and I'll handle mine my way—

(Cindy and Kent enter.)

CINDY: Hi, Mom, Hi, Aunt Faye. You have met Kent, haven't you?

FAYE: Of course, Cindy. Hello, Kent. *(They exchange greetings.)*

CINDY: Mom, anything to eat? We're starved!

CAROLYN *(looking at watch):* Only a half-hour before your father comes home. Dinner will be soon, so better just make it a glass of milk. Can you stay, Kent?

KENT: Thanks, Mrs. Price. Can I use your phone. I'll check at home.

CAROLYN: Of course. *(Kent leaves.)* Cindy, where are Russ and Joan? Weren't you all together?

CINDY: We dropped them off at Joan's. He said he'd call you.

KENT *(reentering):* Would you believe the phone was ringing when I got to the kitchen? It's for you, Mrs. Price.

CAROLYN: Thank you, Kent. I'll be right back. Now, don't any of you touch these lists. *(Leaves.)*

FAYE: Lists! Always lists! How can anybody live that way?

CINDY: Oh, that's just Mom. *(Leaning over table)* Look at this.

FAYE: Watch out. She said not to touch. She'll know if you do.

CINDY: I know; I'm just looking. *(Pointing)* Things to do a month before Christmas. Things to do a week before. Things to do on Christmas Day. This one's marked "Gifts bought." Guess I'd better not look any further.

KENT: Makes Christmas sound pretty cut and dried, doesn't it? Like checking out the stockroom at the grocery store.

FAYE: Maybe her way is better, though. Do you know, I can't find all our Christmas decorations? I tore the house apart yesterday, looking. I'm about ready to fly into a thousand pieces, and your mother is calm and cool as ice cream. Christmas shouldn't make anyone feel that way.

BRAD *(entering):* Well, Faye, how's my favorite sister-in-law? Feel what way?

FAYE: Hello, Brad. You don't really want to know, do you? All I can say is, if the twins change their minds just one more time about what they want for Christmas, I just may lose mine. Those TV commercials have got to go.

KENT: Hi, Mr. Price.

CINDY: Hi, Dad.

BRAD: Good to see you, Kent. Is your mother in the kitchen, Cindy? Dinner sure smells good.

CAROLYN *(reentering):* Right here, Brad. Glad you're home early.

BRAD: You look worried, hon. What's wrong?

CAROLYN: Kent, would you go back and get Russ and Joan? They are coming here with little Donna and Bobby. They'll tell you about it when you get there.

KENT: Sure thing, Mrs. Price. Glad to. *(Leaves.)*

FAYE: What's the trouble, Carolyn?

CAROLYN: It's Joan's father. He's in a hospital in Pittsburgh.

CINDY: A hospital? Oh, no. What's happened to him?

BRAD: He was at a sales meeting there. Was he in an accident?

CAROLYN: They think it's a heart attack. Joan's mother is going to fly there as soon as she can get a flight. I offered to take care of the children while she's gone.

FAYE: What can I do to help, Carolyn?
CAROLYN: I'm trying to think. *(Looks at her lists.)* Cindy and Joan can double up. Russ can sleep on the sofa in the family room; then Donna and Bobby can share his room. But what about Uncle Walt and Aunt Ida?
BRAD: That's right. They're coming on Friday, aren't they?
CAROLYN *(sifting through her lists)*: Flight 209, ten o'clock in the morning. Faye, could you—
FAYE: Put them up? Of course I will. We'll get the old bunk beds down from the attic. The twins will just have to put up with each other again. What else? I'd be glad to—
CAROLYN *(still occupied with her lists)*: I'm—I'm not sure right now. My Christmas isn't quite according to schedule, is it?

(Curtain)

SCENE II

Time: One week later.
Place and Setting: The same, except that an undecorated Christmas tree is added.

(As curtain opens, Joan is seated in chair, with Donna and Bobby standing on either side.)

JOAN: Yes, I talked to Mom last night. She said Daddy will be able to come home next week.
DONNA: Christmas is next week. Will he be here for Christmas?
JOAN: Mom thinks he can come home Christmas Eve. We want to thank God for that, don't we? Won't that be a wonderful Christmas present?
BOBBY: Yes, but what do we do about our other presents?
CAROLYN *(entering)*: What other presents, Bobby?
JOAN: He is talking about our own family's special gifts for Christmas. Mom and Dad always helped us before.
CAROLYN: Well, maybe Brad and I can help you.
BRAD *(entering with box of decorations)*: Help them with what?
CAROLYN: I'm not sure. Joan, what kind of presents are you thinking about? If we go to the store early tomorrow morning, as soon as it opens, maybe we can—

(Russ, Cindy, and Kent enter, carrying various Christmas ornaments and decorations.)

JOAN: Oh, it's not that kind of present, Mrs. Price.

RUSS: Who's talking about presents at this late date?

CAROLYN: Joan and Bobby and Donna seem to need something special for their parents. They'll be home in a few days.

RUSS: Oh, well, if it's something you'd like to make, why don't we go out to the workshop and see what we can do?

CINDY: Why don't we wait and see what they're talking about? I think I know.

KENT: You do? How come you know so much?

CINDY: Joan and I have done a lot of talking the last few nights.

RUSS: I'll say you have! Like a perpetual slumber party. O.K., what kind of presents do you want?

JOAN: It's not what we want, Russ. Isn't that right, Donna?

DONNA *(nodding):* It's what Jesus wants.

KENT: What Jesus wants? I don't get it. What *Jesus* wants?

JOAN: Ever since I can remember, Mom and Dad have asked us at Christmastime to think about what we can give Jesus. Tell him why, Donna.

DONNA: Because Christmas is Jesus' birthday.

RUSS: Of course! *Everybody* knows that!

CINDY: Do you really think everybody *does* know that, Russ? Do you think that everybody you know really thinks about Jesus during Christmastime?

CAROLYN: Maybe we should ask the people—the mob—Faye saw at the shopping center.

KENT: Go on, Joan. Make your point.

JOAN: The point is that Mom and Dad and the three of us always plan a special Christmas birthday party. What do we have at the party, Bobby?

BOBBY: We have a birthday cake for baby Jesus.

RUSS: A birthday cake? What else?

JOAN: We sing some of the Christmas carols we all know, then Mom and Dad and I take turns reading the Christmas chapters in the Bible.

CINDY: We always do that in our Sunday-school pageant. This year I am reading the Christmas story from Luke, about the shepherds.

RUSS: I'm reading about the Wise-men in Matthew.

JOAN: And do you remember what the Wise-men did?

RUSS: They followed the star.

BRAD: They came to Jerusalem asking questions and stirred up some trouble for Herod.

CINDY: They brought gifts to Jesus.

JOAN: That's it, Cindy. After we read about the Wise-men, all of us decide what each one is going to give as our own gift to the Christ child.

BRAD: I don't think that the name of Jesus is on any of your lists, is it Carolyn?

CAROLYN: No. No, it isn't, I'm afraid, Brad.

CINDY: Well, I have been thinking about a gift for Jesus these past few days, since Joan has been here.

KENT: And what did you come up with? How do you give something to Someone like that, who isn't really here? I really don't understand all this. I haven't been to church since I was little. My parents never insisted. They left it up to me.

JOAN: Oh, Kent, that's just what you would have learned in Sunday school. Jesus *is* here, really here. All the time. That is one of His promises. That is one of His gifts to us.

RUSS: I think I'm getting the idea. Kent, there's a place in the Bible that says if you give even a cup of water to someone in Jesus' name, you are giving it to Him. Is that it, Joan?

JOAN: You couldn't be more right, Russ.

KENT: O.K., Joan, so now you and Donna and Bobby have to think of something for this year, right? It must be pretty hard to be thankful to God when your dad is so sick.

JOAN: Yes, I must admit I was pretty upset when we got that first call from the hospital. You know that things like this happen to other people, but it's different when it happens to you. At first, all I could say was, "Why, God, *why?*"

KENT: Did you get any answer?

CINDY: Tell them what you told me the other night, Joan.

JOAN: Well, of course Mother was upset too, but she told me of something else the Bible says: that somehow all things work out together for our good, if we love the Lord. So then I knew that something good would eventually happen, even if we couldn't see it right away.

BRAD: Terrific!

RUSS: Getting back to the main question, did you decide what
    to give Jesus this year?
JOAN: Well, I've thought about it a lot and prayed about it too.
    Our Junior High sponsors at church are a married couple,
    and they had a baby a few months ago. They have had
    trouble getting a baby-sitter for when they have meetings
    and activities. So, well—I thought I'd offer to sit for them,
    if they would want me to. How about you, Donna? Have
    you thought of something you can do?
DONNA: When Mother and Daddy come home, Mother is
    going to be very busy taking care of Daddy, isn't she?
CAROLYN: Yes, Donna, she is. I know your mother will have
    a lot of extra things to do while your dad is getting better.
DONNA: I thought I would help her by keeping my room clean,
    and picking up all my things when I'm through with them.
    I won't wait for Mother to tell me to.
JOAN: That will be quite a change, Donna, and it might not be
    as easy as you think. But I know Mother will be happy to
    have that present. How about you, Bobby?
BOBBY: I can pick up my toys and things, too.
JOAN: Including that big red fire engine you always leave by
    the front door, so Daddy can trip over it?
BOBBY: I'll put that away, too.
JOAN: Good boy, Bobby!
CINDY: I've never done it before, but now I've been planning a
    Christmas gift for Jesus too.
KENT: Are you planning to keep it a secret?
CINDY: No; I'm going to practice my piano lessons every day—
BRAD: I don't believe it!
CINDY: That's right, you'll see. And then I'm going to offer to
    help Mrs. Caine with the music for Junior church. I know
    some of the choruses they sing, and can learn to play them,
    if I work at it. Then Mrs. Caine can attend the regular
    church service sometimes.
CAROLYN: That's a real responsibility, Cindy. I'm sure that
    Mrs. Caine will appreciate your offer to help. But, just
    remember, you can't offer to help and then decide at the
    last minute on Sunday morning not to go, as you have
    been doing. It's not something you can change your mind
    about at the last minute.
CINDY: I know, Mom. That's why it took me so long to think

about it. I know it's not going to be easy to get up on
Sunday morning, when I've been used to sleeping in after
a late date on Saturday night. And the extra practicing
means I may have to miss some of the after-school ac-
tivities. Hope you don't mind, Kent. But I think we can
work things out.

KENT: I don't know, Cindy. This whole idea is new and
strange to me. It doesn't sound like you're giving gifts; it
sounds to me like you're all giving up having a good time.

JOAN: Oh, wow! Is that what it sounds like to you? Because I
don't feel like I'm giving up anything to take care of someone's baby. How about you, Cindy?

CINDY: No, not any more. Joan has helped me to see my piano
practice as a privilege, or a gift from God, rather than a
chore. God has given me a musical talent, and now I'm
going to develop it and use it the way God wants me to.

JOAN: Don't you see, Kent? God loved us so much that He sent
us a Savior. Jesus loved us so much that He was willing to
leave Heaven to be born in the stable of Bethlehem, to live
as a man, and then to die on the cross for our sins. Just
think of that, Kent, the Son of God dying for you and for
me. There would be no hope for any of us otherwise.

BRAD: You're right, Joan. That is God's priceless gift to all of
us. Such great love calls us to love Him and to love each
other with all our hearts and minds and souls.

RUSS: What about the church needing volunteers to help with
some painting at a nursing home?

KENT: Hey, I'm a pretty good painter, if I do say so. Maybe—

JOAN: Wait a minute, Kent, don't volunteer to do something
just because everybody else is doing it. I hope that whatever you decide to do will be because you're thinking about
what Jesus wants to happen in your life.

KENT: If you're going to help with that painting, Russ, count
me in. I'm not sure just what's happening here, but I do
know I want to find out more about Jesus since I've listened to the rest of you talk about all your Christmas gifts.

JOAN: That's a great decision, Kent.

CAROLYN: Maybe I should make a list of all these volunteers—

CINDY (laughing): Oh, Mom! Not another list!

RUSS: Yeah, Mom. I think we can remember.

BRAD: Speaking of lists, though, Carolyn, I've been thinking. You are such a good organizer—

CAROLYN: Why, thank you, dear. A compliment like that is a great Christmas present in itself.

BRAD: What I'm getting at is this. Our young people here have made some pretty important decisions today. Well, how about us? Why don't we give some thought to helping out some way? How about the camp program for the coming year? You're good at planning, and I've had some experience with Cub and Boy Scouts. Church counselors always need help. At least we could look into it.

CAROLYN: Why, I'm ready to give it a try, if you are. Although, a sleeping bag has never been my idea of comfort.

JOAN: Mrs. Price, is it all right if I bake the birthday cake, so we can have it when Dad comes home?

CAROLYN: Of course, Joan. We'd all be happy to celebrate Christmas that way.

BRAD: I think we've all changed our minds about what Christmas should really mean. How about it, kids?

KENT: Just wait till I tell my parents about celebrating the birthday of Jesus with gifts for Him instead of gifts for each other. Can't wait to see their faces.

CAROLYN: Well, I must call Faye and tell her that Christmas doesn't have to mean mobs, madhouses, or even lists.

RUSS: It means sharing Jesus' love with others—

CINDY: It means using your talents the way He wants us to.

JOAN: You know something? Mother was right, wasn't she? All things *do* work together for good to those who love the Lord.

BRAD: Yes, Joan. If you and Bobby and Donna hadn't come to stay with us—Well, our Christmas this year would be just like all our other Christmases—pretty shallow.

RUSS: Your father's heart attack has made us all think with our hearts.

CAROLYN: I don't know about the rest of you, but instead of saying "Merry Christmas" all the time, you know what I feel like saying?

ALL: Happy birthday, Jesus!

BOBBY and DONNA: Happy birthday, baby Jesus!

(Curtain)

Christmas in Word and Song

Velda Blumhagen

Participants: Reader I
Reader II
Adult Chorus (or youth)
Children's Chorus
Mary
Joseph
Shepherds
Wise-men

Setting: The manger scene with Mary, Joseph, manger, and Shepherds should be concealed behind a screen or curtain until the appropriate time in the program.

READER I: God gave us a beautiful world,
    But evil entered in,
      And much of the beauty was destroyed
    Through man's rebellion and sin.

READER II: Down through the years God sent His messengers, the prophets, but man would not listen and turn their hearts back to Him. Yet God still loved the world, and planned to send His own Son to show men His will for them.

ADULT or YOUTH CHORUS: "God So Loved the World"

READER I: It was the prophet Isaiah who gave us the most information about the Redeemer to come. He wrote: "The Lord himself shall give you a sign; Behold, a virgin shall conceive, and bear a son, and shall call his name Immanuel" (7:14). The fulfillment of the prophecies, the coming of God's Son into the world, is the story of Christmas.

READER II: In obedience to the decree of Caesar Augustus, Mary and Joseph made the journey from Nazareth to Bethlehem to be counted for the tax. While they were there the time came for God's Son to be born. The baby was born in a stable and laid in a manger, since there was no room for them in the inn.

READER I: It was in a stable that housed the beasts
That Jesus Christ was born.
Mary wrapped Him in swaddling clothes,
And He slept in a manger that early morn.

(Open curtain to reveal manger scene without Shepherds.)

CHILDREN'S CHORUS: "Away in a Manger"

(Close curtain.)

READER II: Out on the hills near Bethlehem, shepherds were watching their sheep by night, when suddenly an angel of the Lord appeared to them. The glory of God shone upon them as bright as the day, and the hearts of the shepherds quaked with fear.

ADULT or YOUTH CHORUS: "While Shepherds Watched Their Flocks by Night" (stanzas 1 and 2)

READER I: Good tidings indeed did the angel have for them: "I bring you good tidings of great joy, which shall be to all people. For unto you is born this day in the city of David a Saviour, which is Christ the Lord. And this shall be a sign unto you; Ye shall find the babe wrapped in swaddling clothes, lying in a manger" (Luke 2:10-12).

READER II: And so another one of Isaiah's prophecies was fulfilled: "Unto us a child is born, unto us a son is given: and the government shall be upon his shoulder: and his name shall be called Wonderful, Counselor, The mighty God, The everlasting Father, The Prince of Peace" (9:6).

READER I: "And suddenly there was with the angel a multitude of the heavenly host praising God, and saying, Glory to God in the highest, and on earth peace, good will toward men" (Luke 2:13, 14).

ADULT or YOUTH CHORUS: "Hark, the Herald Angels Sing"

READER II: Greatly moved by the wonderful things they had heard and seen, the shepherds hastened to Bethlehem to find the newborn Savior, as the angel had told them. When they found the Child, they explained what had taken place on the hillside. Those who heard wondered at the story, but Mary kept all these things, and pondered them in her heart.

(Open curtain to show the manger scene, with the Shepherds standing or kneeling at the manger.)

CHILDREN'S CHORUS: "Silent Night" (first stanza; joined by Adult Chorus or entire congregation for remainder)

(Close curtain)

READER I: At a later time, Wise-men in the East saw a star. Knowing the prophecies concerning the coming Redeemer, the star was a sign to them that the Savior had come. They came to Jerusalem seeking the newborn King, so that they might worship Him. King Herod sent them to Bethlehem.

READER II: "When they had heard the king, they departed; and, lo, the star, which they saw in the east, went before them, till it came and stood over where the young child was. When they saw the star, they rejoiced with exceeding great joy. And when they were come into the house, they saw the young child with Mary his mother, and fell down, and worshipped him: and when they had opened their treasures, they presented unto him gifts; gold, and frankincense, and myrrh" (Matthew 2:9-11).

(Wise-men enter from rear of sanctuary or auditorium and approach the stage, kneeling there.)

ADULT CHORUS: "We Three Kings of Orient Are"

READER I: Christmas is a time of giving, because God first gave His Son, Jesus. "For God so loved the world, that he gave his only begotten Son, that whosoever believeth in him should not perish, but have everlasting life" (John 3:16).

READER II: Christmas is also a time for receiving the gift of God's love for all: "As many as received him, to them gave he power to become the sons of God, even to them that believe on his name" (John 1:12).

Better Than Moping

Helen C. Shambaugh

This play may be used in conjunction with a traditional program featuring the nativity of Christ, such as the preceding

Cast: Jill, a teen
Don, her brother
Dad
Mother

Time: A few days before Christmas.
Place: A modern-day home.

SCENE I

Setting: A living room with modern furnishings. It appears very messy, with dishes on the coffee table, books and papers scattered about.

(*As scene opens, Don and Jill enter, remove coats, and toss them on the sofa or chair. Don sits on sofa and begins to put feet up on the coffee table and sees the dishes.*)

DON: Oh, brother! Just look at this room! What a mess! It sure isn't like this when Mom is here. Why don't you wash up some of these dishes, Jill?

JILL (*indignantly*): Why don't *I* wash them up? Why don't *you* wash them up if they're in your way? You are the one who used them and carried them in here.

DON: Aw, c'mon. That's women's work.

JILL: Since when? Even Daddy helps Mom do dishes sometimes. Besides, you never do anything around here that is men's work.

DON: Such as what?

JILL: Such as taking out the trash, and such as keeping the walks and driveway clean. So—

DAD *(entering):* What is going on here? *(Removes coat and hat, sits down, and opens newspaper he carried in.)* My goodness! Just look at this room! It's impossible to keep up with both of you. What is your mother going to say when she comes home? She never let you get by with this.

DON: Yeah, I know.

JILL: Well, of all times for Mom to be in the hospital, why does it have to be now? Christmas is only a few days away and nothing is ready.

DON: Yeah, this is the time when Mom always starts to bake all that good stuff, and has the house nice and clean to put up decorations and all. This place never looked like this at Christmastime before.

JILL: And it just doesn't seem the same anyway—so what's the use?

DAD *(putting paper aside and sitting up to look from one to the other):* I can't believe what I'm hearing. To hear you two, one would think your mother is sick and in the hospital by choice!

DON: Aw, Dad, you know we didn't mean it that way.

JILL: Daddy, you know we love Mom. It's just that we miss her and everything she does. Christmas just won't be the same.

DAD: It surely won't be as long as you have that attitude. It certainly doesn't seem to me that either of you miss your mother for the right reasons. She comes home Christmas Eve, you know. Instead of feeling sorry for yourselves and thinking how *your* Christmas is spoiled, what about thinking about her and trying to make her homecoming a happy one?

(Don and Jill look uncomfortable and ashamed.)

DON: Yeah, Dad, guess you're right.

JILL: Well, Daddy, what can we do?

DAD: For openers, Jill, just look around here *(sweeps arm to indicate the room)* and your own room, and then you should be able to think of something. *(Looks at watch.)* As for right now, we had better eat out if we are to get to

the church in time for dress rehearsal. The program is
Christmas Eve, too.

(All begin to leave as curtain closes.)

SCENE II

Time: The next day.
Setting: The same.

(As scene opens, Don and Jill are seated in relaxed positions.)

DON: Jill, I've been thinking about what Dad said last night, and now I feel like a crumb. He is right. We have been acting selfish, anyway, I have.

JILL: I know. I thought about it, too, and feel the same way. I have an idea, though. Let's get Christmas ready for Mom and Dad this year. They have given us a lot of nice ones.

DON: How can we do that? Mom does the baking and Dad always gets the tree.

JILL: Well, Mom isn't here, and won't be until Christmas Eve. Daddy is too busy working and seeing Mom every day to worry about the tree. Why can't we get one ourselves? I have some money, don't you?

DON: Hey, yeah! That's a super idea! We can whip this place into shape—at least better than it is now. We can put up the decorations, I can get the tree, and we can trim it. *(Looks around.)* Yuk! Guess the only way to do it is to clean up some of this mess, so let's start. *(Picks up dishes from coffee table.)*

JILL: O.K. I'll do the kitchen. *(Takes the dishes.)* You do the living room, and then we'll work on the rest of it together.

DON: Sure, and if we hurry, we can have things looking great by the time Mom comes home.

(Jill leaves with the dishes and Don starts picking up papers as curtain closes.)

SCENE III

Time: Christmas Eve.
Setting: The same, but now the room is neat and decorations

are added, including a small tree. The tree is trimmed, with a few packages under it.

(As scene opens, Jill and Don are surveying their work.)

JILL: They should be here soon. Won't Mom be surprised?

DON: She sure will. I'm still worried about that tree. We never had one that small. I didn't realize how expensive Christmas trees are, even artificial ones.

JILL: Don't worry about it Don. I think it is pretty, and I'm sure Mom and Dad will think so too. There aren't many packages, but you know what, Don? I don't even mind that we won't be having gifts to open this year. This was more fun, and it will be so good to have Mom home again. It will be fun just watching her and Daddy open their gifts from us.

DON: Right! It's about time they did a little getting instead of just giving everything to us.

JILL: Yes, you're right. Up to now Christmas was important for what *we* were going to do or get; but now that we planned what we could do for Mom and Dad, things look a lot different.

DON: You noticed that too, huh?

(Door opens and Dad and Mother enter as if from outside. Don and Jill go to her, hug her, and greetings are exchanged.)

MOTHER: Why, Bob, how nice the house looks! It really looks like Christmas in here.

DAD: Well, Ann, none of the credit is mine, I'm afraid. Jill and Don did it all, and I must say I am very proud of them.

MOM: I should say so. When there were no decorations outside, I didn't expect them inside either.

DAD: Well, Ann, I—

DON: Dad was too busy, Mom, and we didn't know how to hook up the outside lights. We didn't want to risk a fire. So we just tried to do our best to give you a nice welcome home.

JILL *(hugging Mother)*: And a Merry Christmas, Mom. I'm so glad you're home again!

MOTHER: And you have. I really don't know what to say. I've been so worried that you would not have a nice Christmas, since I couldn't do any decorating or baking.

JILL: Mom, Daddy made us understand how selfish we were—

DON: Otherwise we'd still be moping around.

JILL: And so we wanted to make it up to you both a little.

DON: But not just for Christmas. We're going to try to do better from now on and help out around here.

MOTHER: What a wonderful Christmas this is going to be. And you two have really done well. *(Looking around)* But there is only one thing wrong with that tree—

DON: It's too small! I knew it!

MOTHER: No, no—it is beautiful. I only meant that it needs more packages under it. Bob, there are some all wrapped, on the shelf in the bedroom closet.

DON: Packages? Mom, you mean there are packages for us, just like other times?

JILL: For us, Mom, really?

MOTHER *(smiling):* Why, of course. I did my Christmas shopping early because I knew I was going to the hospital.

JILL: Oh, Mom, you are tops, and so are you, Dad. But not because of the presents. While we worked and planned for your surprise, we found out that that was more important than our own gifts.

DAD: Well, that is what Christmas is all about, Jill.

DON: Yeah, but it's too bad it took Mom's trip to the hospital to wake us up, though.

DAD: Well, she is home now, and everything is all right, so come on, Don, let's go up and get those packages.

(Dad and Don leave.)

JILL: Mom, the Christmas program is tonight, too. We hate to leave you, but we are all in it.

MOTHER: But you aren't going to leave me. The doctor said I could go as long as I don't overexert. I'll sit in the back and we'll leave as soon as we can.

(Dad and Don reenter carrying packages, which they place under the tree.)

JILL: Don, Mom says she can go to the Christmas program with us.

DON: Great!

DAD: Yes, and *(looking at watch)* I think we had better get going. You two will need time to get into your costumes.

(They begin to put on coats and leave as curtain closes.)

SCENE IV

Time: Later that same evening.
Setting: The same. If stage lights can be operated backstage, the stage may remain darkened and the lights switched on as the family enters.

(As scene opens the family enters and removes coats.)

MOTHER: That was the kind of program I like. It really told the true story of Christmas.

DAD: Yes, that and the carols. There's nothing like the old familiar Christmas carols. They sound more beautiful each year.

DON: Being a shepherd in the program really made me think about the birth of Christ. I mean, it seemed more real. Kneeling there in the stable and at the manger—and it was in a place like that where Jesus came to earth from Heaven. The whole bit—Christmas itself—means more to me now than ever before.

JILL *(softly):* I know what you mean, Don, but it may be that it meant a little more to us this year because we did some growing up. *(Shudders)* When I think of how we spoke to each other just a few days ago—

DON: Yeah, but at first I went along with it because it seemed better than just moping around. But we learned to give instead of just get. God loved the world and He gave. Jesus loved us too, and He gave.

MOTHER *(reflectively):* Well, Don, as your father said, that is what Christmas is all about. That's the spirit of Christmas.

DAD: Yes, and so for our devotions tonight, let's just thank God for giving His Son, and for helping us find the true meaning of Christmas.

(All bow heads as curtain closes.)